Lizards Fo

**Amazing Animal Books
For Young Readers**

By Rachel Smith

Mendon Cottage Books

JD-Biz Publishing

Download Free Books!
http://MendonCottageBooks.com

Read More Amazing Animal Books

Purchase at Amazon.com

Table of Contents

Introduction

Lizards are the favorite creepy-crawly of many children throughout the World. In some areas, they are as easy to find as rocks. Some people even keep them as pets!

Lizard is a very broad term that covers many reptiles, hundreds of kinds, and there are still lizards within rainforests that have yet to be discovered. Whether you're interested in creeping out other people, or just in love with the animal, lizards are interesting to learn about.

From the ones that shoot blood out of their eyes to the ones that blend in with their surroundings, from the large to the small, from the sticky-footed to the claw-footed, lizards fascinate the World over.

What is a lizard?

A lizard is a type of reptile. Reptiles are cold-blooded creatures, meaning that they can't regulate their own temperature in the same way warm-blooded animals (such as mammals, including humans) can. If you put a lizard outside in a winter day in Canada, for example, the air and snow and wind would turn its blood cold and it would die. Reptiles need a warm environment.

A chameleon blending in to its environment

Lizards are members of the Lepidosauria group, excluding snakes and sphenodonts. They are squamate reptiles, meaning that they have scales. Basically, they're the type of reptiles with overlapping scales.

The size of a lizard can be anywhere from chameleons (who can be only a few centimeters) to Komodo dragons, massive animals with a poisonous bite.

Almost all lizards have outer ears, instead of ears inside their heads like snakes. Lizards also have great vision; they are able to see colors and other things very well. Another obvious distinction is that they have legs, whereas snakes do not.

Because lizards are a diverse group, there isn't a lot that can be said about them that is true of all lizards, other than their scales and being a reptile that is not a snake.

Some types of lizards can lose their tail and grow it back; in fact, they tend to lose it on purpose. When a predator tries to eat the lizard, they grab the tail and the tail breaks off, still wriggling in the predator's mouth as the rest of the lizard runs away.

After a few weeks, the lizard's tail will have grown back. It takes many, many genes to have the ability to grow back a tail.

What kinds of lizards are there?

The short answer is there is thousands. Every continent has lizards, minus Antarctica. There are even a lot of species still hidden away in the rainforests that haven't been discovered by the scientific community yet.

A marine iguana

There are four lizard suborders.

The first is Iguania. This covers many lizards, including, as you might have guessed, iguanas. It also includes chameleons, Malagasy iguanas, anoles, American lizards, spiny lizards, and many more.

The second is Gekkota. This doesn't include as many kinds of lizards as Iguania, but it does include all kinds of geckos, including flap-footed lizards as well.

The third is Amphisbaenia, or the worm lizards. These types of lizards look a lot like earthworms, because they are pink and have no limbs. However, they are not snakes, and instead are considered to be members of the lizard family. Very little is known about them, because even the largest ones are only six inches long, and it's very hard to study tiny animals like them.

Lastly, the fourth is Autarchoglossa, which is called a clade and includes snakes. However, it also includes certain kinds of lizards, such as skinks and other types.

Where do lizards live?

In any area they can survive.

A frilled lizard

Lizards live in any environment where they can get enough heat to move and find enough prey to eat. For example, you wouldn't find a living, wild lizard in the Arctic or Antarctica.

However, the lizard is all over the World in all its forms. It can survive in dry environments, and in wet ones, like the rainforest. They live in North America, South America, Asia, Africa, Australia, and other places that allow it to survive.

Lizards tend to be found closer to the equator, which is an imaginary line that is right at the middle of the Earth. The closer the animal is to the equator, the more likely it is that the area will be warm.

Some lizards are at the top of the food chain in their habitat; others are the prey. Some are isolated in islands from the rest of the World, and some are very widespread, both naturally and through human intervention.

The history of lizards and humans

Humans tend to like lizards, though not all of the time. Lizards have never been a big enemy to humans, except in a few cases.

A monitor lizard

Most lizards are too small to bother humans, and very few are very venomous to humans. Even the lizards that are venomous can't kill humans.

There is one major exception to this rule: the Komodo dragon. It is a very big lizard, and has been known to kill people, though infrequently.

Many humans have lizards as pets. They typically keep them in tanks with a warm light and rocks to lay on; most lizards are fed animals such as crickets or even small mice to keep them alive. Lizards enjoy crickets quite a bit.

Lizards aren't nearly as social as mice, and therefore, they don't need to be kept in groups.

Some types of lizards are regularly eaten by people, most notably the iguana in Central America and the spiny-tailed lizard in Africa. The lizard is also food for some nomadic tribes in Africa. Lizards are often said to taste like chicken.

What is a gecko?

Geckos belong to the suborder Gekkota. They live in places that are warm.

A leopard gecko

This type of lizard can't blink, because it has no eyelids, so to keep their eyes from drying out, they lick them. It's a transparent membrane that covers their eyes. They also have far better color vision than humans and can see colors that humans can't.

Geckos are a very diverse group, with over 1,500 kinds of geckos out there. Some are nocturnal (sleep during the day, active at night) and

---

others are diurnal (sleep during the night, active during the day, like humans).

Unlike most lizards, geckos make an unusual sound to communicate: chirping. It's a softer sound, and the name for geckos comes from a word meant to mimic the sound they make.

The largest species of gecko, which lived in New Zealand, was wiped out in the 19th century when rats and other vermin were introduced to the islands; many other animals died out this way.

The smallest species of gecko lives on a small island off the coast of the Dominican Republic, and it's generally less than two centimeters long. It hasn't had the same problem as the largest geckos did, and still flourishes in its native habitat.

Geckos are the most colorful kind of lizards; they come in all patterns and colors. Some can even change colors depending on the time of day.

Some geckos can have babies without a mate.

All geckos shed their skin regularly. For example, the leopard gecko tends to shed its skin every two or four weeks. Geckos will typically help their shedding along, by removing the old skin and eating it.

Many types of geckos can stick to almost any surface, due to adhesive pads on their feet. They do this without liquid or tiny hooks.

Geckos also have about a hundred teeth, and they replace them completely every three to four months. There is always a replacement tooth next to the current tooth.

What is a Komodo Dragon?

Komodo dragons are the largest of the lizards, some being up to 10 feet long! They also always weigh over a hundred pounds. And they do not play nicely with humans.

A Komodo Dragon

The Komodo dragon lives in four islands in Indonesia. Since there are no other major predators on the islands, the Komodo dragon is the equivalent of a tiger or a bear in the food chain. It eats what it wants, when it wants.

While death by Komodo dragon is very rare, it has been known to go after humans. Its bite is full of germs and toxins, and that often is what kills the victim, not the bite itself.

A Komodo dragon is also called a Komodo monitor, but not usually.

They have tails as long as their bodies, and serrated (jagged-edged) teeth, which are replaced pretty regularly. Because their teeth are mostly covered by their gums, they tend to cut them eating, and so there is frequently blood coming from their mouth. This is perfect for all the little bacteria that live in its mouth.

They also have armored skin, with bone like little plates making their skin like chain mail. It is very hard to damage a Komodo dragon.

A Komodo dragon doesn't typically hunt prey, at least not all the time. They will usually go for prey that's already dead, though they will hunt down prey too. When they attack, they usually ambush from a hidden spot and go for the throat.

A Komodo dragon's sense of smell is very good; they can pick up dead animals from miles away. They are also messy eaters, tearing off huge pieces off of carcasses and swallowing it whole while they hold onto the prey with their forelegs.

They can even swallow smaller prey whole, such as a goat, because they have flexible jaws and very expandable stomachs. When they've digested all the good parts of a meal, they spit up the bad parts, in what's called a gastric pellet.

A Komodo dragon often moves to sunlight to digest, because if the food they eat is undigested too long, it could go bad and make the lizard sick.

Because a Komodo dragon has such a slow metabolism (which is how fast they use calories), they can survive on as little as 12 meals a year. They tend to eat their body weight in food when they do eat.

The climate for a Komodo dragon must be warm and dry. Like most lizards, they depend on outside heat to keep their blood warm and to have energy.

They mate in roughly September, and males typically fight for a female's attention by standing on their hind legs and grappling with each other.

Komodo dragons lay eggs, and the way the mother cares for them is that she either uses an old nest, or digs up one herself. Then she lays the eggs and incubates them for seven or eight months.

Baby Komodo dragons live in trees and feed on insects; they have to keep out of reach of other predators and especially adult Komodo dragons, who might try to eat them.

Sometimes, a female Komodo dragon can have babies without a male. It's very rare, and the babies tend to be males. This is known as parthenogenesis.

Komodo dragons have a hierarchy (set up of who's in charge). The larger the Komodo dragon, the sooner he gets to eat. Sometimes similar sized dragons will fight each other over it, and the victors have been known to eat the losers.

Scientific studies prove that similar lizards lived in places like Australia long ago, perhaps millions of years in the past, but they were wiped out by changing environment. The Komodo dragons that live on the little islands in Indonesia have managed to live through many different changes.

The Komodo dragon has only known to Western scientists since 1910, a little more than a hundred years ago. Since then, they have been in zoos as great attractions.

Komodo dragons are considered vulnerable to endangerment. There are about 5,000 in the wild, and hunting them is not allowed.

What is an iguana?

Iguana' refers to two species: the green iguana, and the Lesser Antillean iguana. Its name is derived from the Taino (native Cuban people) word iwana.

A very green iguana

Unlike other groups of lizards, the iguana is herbivorous, meaning that it eats plants.

It has a tympanum (an ear drum) behind its eye, and is often very hard to spot in its natural habitat. Iguanas have a dewlap (which is like a loose piece of skin that hands from the chin and down the neck) and spikes on their bodies.

Iguanas also have subtympanic shields to protect their tympanums, and have a 'third eye' in the middle of their forehead. It's a pale scale that actually picks up a lot of things, such as whether it's daytime or not. It's different from an iguana's regular eyes, however.

The green iguana (also known as the common iguana, or its scientific name, *Iguana Iguana*) is very large. It can reach several feet in length from head to tail. It is also commonly green, but not always. Sometimes, a green iguana will have a reddish hue to it, or other colors, such as black, pink, lavender, blue, and more.

It is a native from the South of Mexico to Brazil and beyond; it's been added to Florida, Puerto Rico (where it's considered more of a danger to the local animals) and other places in North and Central America and the Caribbean.

Green iguanas are the kind that most people are familiar with as pets. They have a calm nature, and are pretty easy to handle. However, due to their size, they tend to be harder to care for in that way, pet owners have to make sure the tank is big enough and that the heater keeps it warm. The problem with keeping the green iguana as a pet is that they are often misfed. For example, some will feed them meat or meat-based foods, which the iguana will eat, but will kill the iguana within a couple of years. Iceberg lettuce is also often fed to iguana pets, but the problem is that iceberg lettuce has next to no nutrition in it. Good foods for iguanas include leafy plants such as dandelions, kale, and mustard greens.

A green iguana has several things going for it to keep it protected from predators. For starters, the spikes on its back can harm something trying to grab it or bite it. Next is its muscular tail; it can whip predators with it, and it is quite painful. Lastly, their tail can also break off if it's grabbed, so that the iguana can get away.

They have very sharp, leaf-shaped, and serrated teeth. They can shred plants and human skin easily. It's kind of similar to some kinds of dinosaur teeth (herbivores, or plant eaters).

A female green iguana can lay up to 71 eggs in one nesting time. Green iguana females in the same area are synchronized to lay eggs at the same time. However, a female green iguana isn't much of a mom; once she's laid the eggs, she leaves them.

Female green iguanas sometimes lay their eggs among alligator nests, so that they will be protected by the more caring mother alligator.

Interestingly, the male green iguana, in a family group, will protect female iguanas with their own bodies. No other lizard does this.

The Lesser Antillean iguana is the other lizard in this family. It lives in the Lesser Antilles, which is a group of small islands in the

Caribbean. It's a little different from green iguanas, in that it doesn't have the stripes on its tail that green iguanas have, or the round large scale below the ear that its cousin has as well.

It's also usually gray, and has a shorter, blockier face than the green iguana.

What is a horny toad?

The horny toad, despite its name, is not a toad. It is a lizard.

A horny toad

The horny toad lives in North America, and its real name is the horned lizard. For obvious reasons, it is called both the horny toad and the horny frog; its body looks a lot like a toad's, except for the tail.

The horned lizards are a genus, and there are about 15 species, with 8 of them in the United States of America. They are very distantly related to the Australian thorny devil.

A few things they have in common with the Australian thorny devil is that they prey upon ants, and that their strategy for getting prey is more of a stay and wait kind of strategy. It is suggested by some that they evolved from the same animal, just ended up in different areas and therefore ended up different.

Horned lizards are also prey. Their coloring and horniness helps them blend in to the landscape; if they are spotted, something they do to confuse the predator is to run a quick, short burst, and then stop suddenly, hopefully making the predator lose sight of them.

Lastly, these are the lizards that squirt blood from their eyes. They do this by making less blood leave the head than enters, and this breaks the blood vessels and allows them to shoot blood. Animals like coyotes and ocelots find the taste foul; it doesn't usually bother birds that are trying to eat the lizard.

The horned lizard is the state reptile of Wyoming.

Why aren't frogs, toads, alligators, and crocodiles lizards?

Let's start with frogs and toads.

A great treefrog

Frogs and toads are amphibious, meaning they can live in the water as well as on the land. This is something that lizards can't do; while many types can swim, they can't actually live in the water.

Frogs and toads also are not reptiles; they are amphibians, which are said to be the first animals to leave the water in evolution. They have thin, moist skin, and they can't be far from water for too long, or else their skin will dry out. They are simply very different animals.

So, why aren't alligators and crocodiles called lizards?

They belong to the order Crocodilia, which includes alligators, crocodiles, caimans, gharials, and false gharials. All of these animals are semi-aquatic, which lizards are not. Again, while lizards swim, they don't generally do their hunting in the water, whereas these animals do. In fact, a crocodile might stay in the water all day waiting for prey, looking like a log.

Crocodiles found in a zoo

There are some similarities, to be sure. Crocodilia are also reptiles, and they eat meat. However, the crocodile, the gharial, and all the rest, are simply not structured in a similar way to lizards.

A crocodile has some difficulty outside of the water; their size makes them unwieldy, whereas lizards are usually fastest on land as compared to water.

The crocodile also has a different build; its jaws are made to have the most power and grip slamming down on prey, whereas the lizard's mouth is a bit more like a human's, though usually with more teeth. The crocodile is a reptile that has been around far longer than all kinds of lizards, and it will probably outlast them all.

Conclusion

Lizards are pretty cool. They can do things that a lot of other animals can't, and they can make very interesting pets. Leopard geckos and green iguanas are the most common lizard pets, but that doesn't mean you can't observe lizards in your backyard, if you live in a warm climate.

If it weren't for lizards, we would have far more pests. For instance, Komodo dragons balance their home's ecosystem by eating excess prey animals. Horned lizards eat ants and other bugs that may bother us.

Without lizards, we wouldn't have the beautiful geckos to look at, or the intimidating green iguana to stare down.

A World without lizards would continue, but every animal matters. Just because no one would miss the tiniest chameleon doesn't mean we shouldn't be on the lookout to keep their habitats safe.

Many lizards nowadays are threatened by human growth and the destruction of their habitats, just like so many animals throughout the world. Hopefully, we will be able to find a way to live in peace with the lizards, so that both humans and lizards can flourish.

Author Bio

Rachel Smith is a young author who enjoys animals. Once, she had a rabbit who was very nervous, and chewed through her leash and tried to escape. She had pet fish, including a pink kissing gourami that liked to eat the other fish. She's also had several pet mice, who were the funniest little animals to watch. She lives in Ohio with her family and writes in her spare time.

Our books are available at

1. Amazon.com

2. Barnes and Noble

3. Itunes

4. Kobo

5. Smashwords

6. Google Play Books

Download Free Books!
http://MendonCottageBooks.com

Publisher

JD-Biz Corp

P O Box 374

Mendon, Utah 84325

http://www.jd-biz.com/

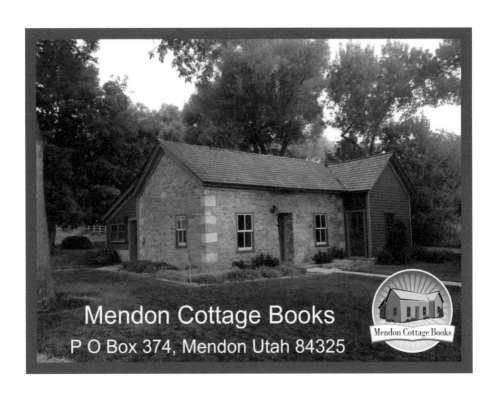

Printed in Great Britain
by Amazon